BETTE DAVIS

A Life from Beginning to End

Copyright © 2019 by Hourly History.

Table of Contents

Introduction
Early Life
From Acting School to Hollywood Success
Bette's First Husband and the Oscar Award
Jezebel
Success with Warner Brothers
A New England Romance
Now, Voyager and All About Eve
The Horror Years
The Feud with Joan Crawford
My Mother's Keeper
Conclusion

Introduction

Bette Davis is generally regarded as one of the most prominent and versatile actresses of the twentieth century. She started her career by doing theater in New York, where a Universal Studios talent scout spotted her and sent her to Hollywood. Universal offered her a contract and a few Grade C movies, but the question was, what to do with Bette Davis? She was talented and could act, but she was no conventional Hollywood beauty and could only be described as volatile and argumentative.

Davis was indeed argumentative enough to demand better roles, and eventually, she got them. Her best-known movies include *Of Human Bondage*, *Jezebel*, and *Dark Victory*. Middle age spelled the end for many female careers in Hollywood—but for Bette Davis, it simply meant another beginning. From *All About Eve* to *What Ever Happened to Baby Jane*, Davis continued to star in successful movies almost up to her death. When she wasn't making films, she appeared on television and wrote memoirs. Work was her life.

Still, Bette Davis managed to get married four times and have one natural daughter and two adopted children. While Bette loved her family, her career always came first, a fact which was to the detriment of her husbands, who did not enjoy their status as "Mr. Davis." Later in life, her daughter B. D. wrote a scathing biography of her mother, describing Bette as an abusive alcoholic. Bette never forgave her, nor did she understand the criticism. She had always worked to support her family.

As she got older, Bette Davis suffered from breast cancer and several strokes. She died in France on October 6, 1989, at the age of 81. Her tombstone, which reads "She did it the hard way," aptly describes Bette Davis's six-decades-long career.

Chapter One

Early Life

"Before that performance, I wanted to be an actress. When it ended, I had to be an actress."

—Bette Davis

Ruth Elizabeth Davis was born on April 5, 1908, nine months to the day following her parents' wedding in Lowell, Massachusetts. Bette frequently joked that no one could accuse her parents, both 21 years of age, of having a shotgun wedding; she'd definitely been born within the bounds of legitimacy. In conservative New England, that was important.

Her father, Harlow Davis, had raged against his wife's pregnancy from the start. The last thing he wanted was a child, and he accused his wife, Ruth Augusta, of severe carelessness. He never forgave Ruthie for getting pregnant and never fully accepted their daughter. Harlow Davis was known to be disagreeable and irresponsible. His own family had warned Ruthie against the marriage, and when Bette's sister Barbara, known as "Bobby," arrived less than two years later, Harlow reacted with the same tantrum, again blaming his wife. Theirs was not a happy household.

In 1909, Harlow graduated from Harvard Law School and began working in the patent department of a shoe manufacturer. He was seldom home, and Ruthie became despondent from spending so much time alone with two young children to take care of. Another large part of her depression was due to Harlow's frequent infidelities. Meanwhile, both Bette and Bobby tried desperately to please their father, but Harlow remained cold and distant. He simply wasn't interested in establishing a relationship with them. He never would be.

Bette was eight years old when her parents finally divorced. Although her younger sister was overwhelmed by the news, Bette bid her father farewell at the railway station by dancing, cheering, and clapping loudly. The sarcastic nature for which she was famed as an adult obviously developed early. She wouldn't miss her father. Now, there would finally be some peace at home. In order to support her daughters, Ruthie worked as a governess and did a bit of photography on the side. She was still young and attractive and was rarely short of male attention. Bette and Bobby, however, vetoed all her suitors. They had no desire for a second father. It wasn't until years later that Bette realized how they had shortchanged their mother of any possible happiness.

As Ruthie did her utmost to earn money for her family in New York, the girls were sent to a boarding school on a farm in western Massachusetts. There, they would spend the better part of six years, taking care of the farm animals, cooking, sewing, and learning to read and write. It was a spartan and rugged life to be sure—and a big adjustment for two young girls from the city. Still, Bette would come to love their long days spent outside and their evenings by the fire.

In 1921, Ruthie took a step up in her photography career by moving her family to New York City and enrolling in the Clarence White School of Photography. Here, in the city that never sleeps, Bette began high school. A budding young woman, she knew little about sex as her puritanical mother refused to discuss the subject, so when Bette was kissed for the first time at age 14, she worried that she might become pregnant. When she had her first period, she assumed she was dying. At that point, Bette demanded a talk with her mother, who finally cleared up a few misconceptions.

Ruthie was unable to afford college for her girls, so she sent them to the coeducational Cushing Academy in Northfield, Massachusetts. The trio was forced to move again. It was at the Cushing Academy that the teenaged Bette met Harmon "Ham" Nelson, who would later become her first husband. She was madly infatuated with the handsome boy who played with the band at the school's dances. Her imagination ran rampant with visions of a perfect home with the perfect white picket fence. As with most teenagers, however, young love proved to be fickle. When Ham left for college, Bette transferred her affections to another boy, Fritz. She still dreamed of that perfect home and merely switched the man of the house from Ham to Fritz. It was a pattern that would repeat itself throughout Bette's life.

It was in no man's power to captivate Bette's indomitable spirit—only the theater could do that. The first play Bette ever saw was Ibsen's *The White Duck* at Boston's Repertory Theater. She was 18 years old and utterly enthralled. Before even leaving the theater, she knew exactly what she would do with the rest of her life. Bette Davis would be an actress. And not just any actress— she was going to be the best actress of all time. When Ruthie enthusiastically wrote to Harlow about their daughter's new plans, he scornfully replied that she should become a secretary instead. "Betty will never be a successful actress," he wrote. "She doesn't have what it takes." Her father's rejection continued to be a disappointment to Bette, but it would serve as an inspiration as well. Bette Davis, as obstinate as ever, was determined to prove Harlow wrong, and her greatest supporter Ruthie would help her in that endeavor.

In 1927, Ruthie took Bette to New York without explaining what she had in mind. The fact that they took a cab from Grand Central Station told Bette that whatever meeting they were going to had to be extremely important. The cab took them to the John Murray Anderson School of Theater and Dance on the Upper Eastside. It was a prestigious school that counted dancer Martha Graham among its teachers. Ruthie admitted to Mr. Anderson that she couldn't afford the tuition but promised she would pay him back in the future if he took Bette on as a student. Anderson himself was never quite sure why he agreed to the deal, but as luck would have it, he did.

Leaving Bobby up north with friends, Ruthie and Bette moved to New York. With Ruthie, Bette would always come first, which caused serious consequences for Bobby in later years. Young Bette Davis, who had always seen herself as the star of the family with Bobby merely playing a supporting role, was on the road to a career as a professional actress.

Chapter Two

From Acting School to Hollywood Success

"They dumped me. My career was almost over before it had really begun."

—Bette Davis

Bette enjoyed her time at the Anderson school. There, she learned for the first time how to move properly and how to interact with an audience. She especially enjoyed her classes with Martha Graham, who taught her how to fall without getting hurt and how to ascend and descend a staircase with grace. It was also at Anderson that Bette learned to speak clearly and lose her noticeable Boston accent. The future actress Joan Blondell was one of her classmates, although Bette rarely socialized, spending all her energies on her studies.

During this time, Fritz, now a senior at Yale, proposed to her. Bette, awe-struck by the diamond ring he presented to her, told Fritz she would think about it, but ultimately, the choice would be easy. Fritz became history as soon as he demanded that she give up the theater. Now that she had a plan and a foot in the door, nothing was going to stop her pursuing her dream. Besides, Bette had just received a letter from her old love, Ham.

While she renewed her relationship with Ham, Bette worked hard at perfecting her acting skills. Anderson offered a $250 scholarship for the most promising student at the end of the first term, and knowing how hard her mother was working to support her, Bette was determined to win this princely sum. Her lead role in *The Famous Mrs. Fair* seemed like the perfect opportunity to showcase her talent and win the scholarship. Bette focused hard on the role, but two days before the performance, she developed a serious case of the flu. She could barely talk, much less emote to an audience. Ruthie, always the supportive mother, purchased all the available cold medicines and took time off work to try to heal her daughter as quickly as possible.

On the day of the performance, Bette made it—barely—through the first two acts of the play. When she came off stage, her body began to shake, as did her voice, which became hoarser and hoarser. As far as Bette was concerned, she had not only lost any chance at a scholarship, but she would probably be kicked out of Anderson's.

Yet by a stroke of luck, the character of Mrs. Fair ages from an energetic young girl to an older, bitter woman during the course of the play. In perfect unison, Bette the actress fell apart at the same time as the character of Mrs. Fair was aging and also falling apart. The audience and the teachers were stunned that a beginning student could show such a wide range of acting ability. A few days later, a surprised Bette became the recipient of the sought-after scholarship. Ironically, she would never use it.

Soon afterward, Bette was offered a professional acting part with the Provincetown Playhouse. Accepting would mean leaving the safety of school behind and entering the world of real theater. She discussed her dilemma with Mr. Anderson, who immediately advised her to take the part, the first professional acting job in her career. Following his advice, Bette accepted the role and left school behind. To her great disappointment, however, the start of the play was postponed for three months. She couldn't go back to school and spent the time in limbo. It was a restless time, but when the play, *The Earth Between,* finally went on, her reviews were good.

Shortly after, Bette received a call from the Repertory Theater asking if she would be interested in replacing the current actress playing Hedwig in *The Wild Duck* following the end of *The Earth Between.* This was the very play that had drawn Bette to the theater in the first place, and she accepted without hesitation. Opening night brought one of the most thunderous applause in the theater's history. The play was a smash hit. As Bette was the newest member of the cast, the lead actress led her on stage alone for a solo curtain call. The audience cheered and waved, and Bette later recalled that this was when she realized that she had "found the one true, enduring romance in my life."

Bette had become theater news. Now recognized as an up-and-coming actress, she had no issues getting starred in new plays and made her debut on Broadway in 1929. She wasn't getting paid much, and her father rarely sent money to support the family, but Bette didn't mind. She was on her way.

While she was performing in *Solid South* in 1930, a talent agent from Universal Studios arranged for a screen test. The result was a three-month contract at $300 a week—excellent money at the time. Universal would pay for round-trip train tickets for both Bette and Ruthie, but the talent agent added that he seriously doubted that she would make a success of it as a starlet since she looked very different from the usual dime-a-dozen blond and curvy Hollywood actress. Bette quickly retorted, "I wasn't planning to be a starlet. I was planning to be a star."

After leaving the Broadway stage for Hollywood, many actors claim to miss live performances. Bette never did. To her, shows ran for a finite length of time and then were done. Movies, however, would last forever. At the time, while sitting on a westbound train, Bette had no idea how long her forever would be. When she arrived in Tinseltown after the five-day journey, she was a rarity among the local females. At the age of 23, Bette was a devoted Puritan and a virgin. She was immediately made aware that she wasn't the typical Hollywood glamour type when the studio representative failed to find her on the platform because "he didn't see anyone who looked like an actress."

Following the filming of her first movie, *Bad Sister*, Bette overheard the head of production at Universal saying that "she has as much sex appeal as Slim Summerville." The rejection took a toll on her ego. In truth, many Hollywood people simply disliked Broadway people. A fellow actor in *Bad Sister*, another newbie from Broadway called Humphrey Bogart, was also ridiculed on the set.

Despite her initial difficulties, Bette's contract was renewed. She quickly realized that the Hollywood system was pretty much a slave-system, with the major studios in complete control of every facet of the actors' lives. But if there was anything worse than having a contract, it was not having a contract. She accepted the terms even though she was virtually helpless to make any decisions about her career or the movies she was cast in.

Following *Bad Sister,* Bette had a minuscule part in the film *Seed.* In total, she would make six pictures for Universal before she was let go. Her Hollywood career seemed over before it had taken off. Bette was heartbroken. Making movies had been fun for her, and she felt like she had failed at the one thing she wanted to do most in life. In addition, without a contract, there would be no more money coming in. Dejected, she and Ruthie packed their belonging for the return trip to New York.

They had just finished their packing when the phone rang. The caller identified himself as George Arliss, the British actor and filmmaker who had found success in Hollywood. Bette had no reason to believe the famed actor would be calling and assumed it was a friend having fun at her expense. After several sarcastic remarks, she realized to her horror that the caller was indeed George Arliss and that he was looking for a female lead in his next movie, *The Man Who Played God.* He asked her to come to Warner's Studio as quickly as she could.

It was late 1931 when Bette met with Arliss, who had the generosity not to mention her sarcastic phone behavior. He asked her questions about herself, and she told him about her meager but successful stage career. Before leaving, she had secured the leading female role in his latest movie. She attempted to act dignified, but inside

Bette was jumping with joy. Arliss not only revived her almost non-existent Hollywood career, but he also arranged for her to be under contract with Warner Brothers—a five-year contract at $400 a week.

When *The Man Who Played God* premiered, Bette Davis became an instant success, and in Hollywood, success meant being treated like royalty in a castle where all doors opened. Bette had entered the land of magic.

Chapter Three

Bette's First Husband and the Oscar Award

"Mr. Arliss not only kept me in Hollywood and saved my screen career, but he also gave me the opportunity to get a Warner Brothers contract. And you know what that led to! I became known as 'The Fourth Warner Brother.'"

—Bette Davis

While Bette was making headway in Hollywood, her relationship with Ham had been on and off. Ruthie pointed out that she had to make a decision—or risk becoming an old maid. Bette, still a virgin, agreed. She and Ham were subsequently married on August 18, 1932, in Yuma, Arizona. They moved into a cottage in Hollywood while Bette made her Warner Brothers movies.

Their marriage was fraught with tension from the start. Ham had married one woman but ended up with three as Bette, Ruthie, and Bobby were never far apart. His career as a musician wasn't taking off while Bette was doing steady work. The discrepancy in pay between husband and wife was frequently pointed out in the press, and Ham refused to let Bette buy a proper house until he could afford to pay for it. It was only going to become more challenging.

In 1934, Bette signed her second contract with Warner Brothers, this one for seven years at double her salary. With Greta Garbo and Katharine Hepburn being labeled "box office poison," Bette was well-positioned to become one of Warner's leading stars. That same year, RKO was casting for Summerset Maugham's *Of Human Bondage*. Bette longed to play the female lead role of boorish waitress Mildred Rogers. She begged and pleaded with Jack Warner until he agreed to lend her out to RKO. Leslie Howard played the sensitive, club-footed medical student Philip, who falls in love with Mildred.

The major themes in *Of Human Bondage* are the cruelties of which humans are capable. As a boy, Philip was bullied because of his foot. Bullying and torture invariably involve power by someone dominant over a submissive person. In *Of Human Bondage,* Philip feels weak as a result of his club foot. He creates his own torture by remaining bonded to the cruel Mildred. He lacks any type of control over his passion for her as they play their sadomasochistic games and is only freed from bondage after her death.

Knowing the Hollywood studios' penchant for showing their actresses at their best, Bette insisted on doing her own makeup as the character of Mildred deteriorates in health. She was brave enough to make herself look haggard. To her, it didn't make sense that a dying, sick woman would look her best on her deathbed. The reality of illness and poverty are stark, and Bette wanted to convey that message. In doing this, Bette chose her craft over her vanity. She was to do the same decades later when filming *What Ever Happened to Baby Jane*. Bette, Ham, and Ruthie nervously awaited the reviews following the movie's release. How would the audients react to the grim reality of cruelty and death? The story itself, while riveting, is an unpleasant one.

Of Human Bondage opened at Radio City Music Hall on June 28, 1934. The reviewers raved. The movie was an instant success. The executives at Warner Brothers were miffed, however, that one of their own had made this acclaimed movie for another studio and that RKO was getting the credit. They did their best to exclude *Of Human Bondage* from any official promotional literature about Bette.

Everyone assumed Bette would be a shoo-in for an Oscar nomination. She was, however, ignored. Claudette Colbert ultimately won the Best Actress award that year for *It Happened One Night*. Yet Bette would not have to wait long to get her hands on the coveted Academy Award. In 1935, after her performance as Joyce Heath in *Dangerous*, she won the first of what would be two Oscars. For the rest of her life, Bette claimed to have been the one who gave the award its popular nickname; she said she started calling the statue Oscar since it reminded her of her husband, whose middle name was Oscar.

By now, Bette was well-known and respected in all realms of the film industry. Warner Brothers was a known star-maker, and its entire publicity department worked to put Bette's name in the limelight. A few years after *Dangerous*, she was one of the many actresses considered for the coveted role of Scarlett O'Hara in *Gone with the Wind*. Losing that part to Vivien Leigh was to be one of Bette's major regrets.

By 1938, a frustrated Ham Nelson demanded a divorce while Bette was shooting her next blockbuster, *Jezebel*. His reason? As stated in the divorce paper, she read too much! He said she "read to an unnecessary degree" and that "it was all very upsetting." Years later, Bette admitted that, amongst other things, it was her romantic relationship with Howard Hughes which contributed to the failure of the marriage. Ham never made that fact public.

Chapter Four

Jezebel

"I love my profession. I would never stop. Relax? I relax when I work. It's my life."

—Bette Davis

In 1933, *Jezebel* had been a successful Broadway play with Miriam Hopkins playing the title character. When Warner Brothers turned it into a movie five years later, Hopkins naturally assumed she would replay her role as the beautiful southern Jezebel. After all, Miriam was beautiful, southern, and a natural for the part of the spoiled heiress. Director William Wyler decided on Bette Davis instead, and she was neither beautiful nor southern. Wyler saw what others didn't, and this was to be the defining role of Bette's early career, catapulting her from starlet to star. Bette and Willie Wyler would enjoy an affair during the duration of the film, and when she found herself pregnant, the paternity of the baby was uncertain. Bette opted to get an abortion.

Jezebel has frequently been compared to *Gone with the Wind*, which was released a year later. Both films have headstrong but flawed female leads. Both Scarlett O'Hara and *Jezebel's* Julie Marsden are spoiled coquettes, indifferent to the opinion of others. Chivalry and manners form the backbone of both stories. *Jezebel* is a more accurate description of the antebellum south; instead of master and slaves enjoying a familial relationship as depicted in *Gone with the Wind*, in *Jezebel*, slaves wait on their masters.

Jezebel is set in New Orleans prior to the American Civil War. Bette's character Julie enjoys being contrary and makes fun of the proper manners that are expected of a young lady. She is habitually and deliberately late, even to her own engagement party. Independent and capricious, Julie flirts with her ex-beau, Buck Cantrell, to ensure the attention of her fiancé, Preston Dillard.

Determined to make a splash at the annual Olympus Ball, Julie decides, against all precedent, to wear a bold red dress at an affair that allows young ladies to wear only white. Preston is furious but takes her to the ball anyway. The moment they enter, Julie understands she has gone too far. The entire room is abuzz at this scarlet apparition. Not a soul approaches her and Preston, and they face plenty of cold shoulders. While there is hardly any conversation, Bette's face reflects the moment to perfection. This social gaffe is bigger than Julie intended, and Bette's eyes tell the whole story. When she begs Preston to take her home, he refuses. He forces her to dance and make a social spectacle of herself. Only after she has been suitably humiliated does he take her home, and then he breaks up with her before going up north.

The conflict in the story is not between Julie and Preston—it is between Julie and herself. She recognizes she is in the wrong and tries to amend her behavior. She comes to understand that her recklessness is responsible for her unhappiness, and Bette plays the shift in character very well. During Preston's absence, she behaves with utter decorum to regain her shattered reputation. She plays games with the slave children and becomes aware of the social inequities for the first time in her life. She begins to take responsibility for her behavior. Bette's portrayal of remorse and redemption is understated and powerful.

When Preston returns, Julie can't wait for him to see the new, improved Julie Marsden. However, when he arrives at a picnic, he coldly introduces Julie to his new wife. As deadly yellow fever soon takes its toll on the citizens of New Orleans, Preston is infected. Knowing that he will soon die, Julie joins him on the transport wagon to an island where he will be quarantined, ostensibly to offer comfort. Truthfully, she knows he will die and that she will also be dead soon. She finds redemption in making the ultimate sacrifice—her own life.

The role of Julie is a challenging balancing act between being flighty and being tough and resolute. Bette manages to carry each scene with all the necessary nuances. She is brilliant. The role of Jezebel earned Bette her second Oscar.

As good as the movie is, it was rushed through production. Warner Brothers was aware that MSM was planning on making *Gone with the Wind*, and they were eager to get *Jezebel* out first. They succeeded by three months. David O. Selznick of MGM was infuriated and actually threatened to sue for unfair trade practices. The one huge error Warner Brothers made in rushing the movie through production was to film it in black and white, especially considering the importance of the red dress. *Gone with the Wind*, of course, would be shown in glorious color.

It was around this time that Bette entered into an affair with millionaire Howard Hughes. They had first met at the Tailwaggers ball, a benefit dinner for an animal rescue organization for which Bette was president. That evening, she wore a pink gown with a very deep neckline. Like her red gown in the movie, this dress was meant to attract serious attention. She immediately caught the eye of Hughes; his love of cleavage was well known. Bette was unapologetically on the prowl. She and Ham had not been sexually compatible, with Bette wanting more than Ham was prepared to give. During the evening, Bette and Hughes were photographed together, and since she was still married, the photos caused an international stir. At the end of the night, Hughes asked if he might call her.

They attempted to keep their get-togethers discrete, meeting at a house in Malibu. Ham became aware of these dates, and so did the papers. In October of 1938, radio personality Walter Winchell hinted that Bette and Hughes might get married following the necessary legal proceedings of a divorce, but the affair soon ran its course.

Chapter Five

Success with Warner Brothers

"With success, you go everywhere first-class, and you aren't dependent on others. You don't have to wait around anymore. People wait for you. But one thing success does not guarantee is happiness, although as Joe Mankiewicz said, 'Happiness doesn't buy money.'"

—Bette Davis

If *Jezebel* qualifies as a tear-jerker, Bette's next movie, *Dark Victory,* was positively torrential. It was promoted as a "woman's movie," but it transcends that. The year of 1939 was an emotional one for Bette. She won an Oscar for *Jezebel,* ended her marriage and her affairs with Howard Hughes and director William Wyler while consoling herself with an affair with her latest co-star, George Brent. Her divorce brought her to a near nervous breakdown, but work had always seen her through bad times, so she grasped at the opportunity to do *Dark Victory.*

Dark Victory could have been a cliché—a beautiful girl is dying and falls for her doctor. It might have remained a cliché if not for Bette, who brought considerable depth to the character of the spoiled heiress, Judith Traherne. Like Julie in *Jezebel*, Judith is initially spirited and thoughtless.

All she cares about are her horses and herself, and she's not above using a horse crop on someone to get what she wants. Unexplained headaches lead her to a doctor's visit. It turns out Judith suffers from a brain tumor and does not have long to live. George Brent plays the dashing Dr. Frederick Steele, who falls in love with Judith and, in an effort to spare her feelings, tries to hide her fatal illness from her. But, of course, she finds out. She is slowing going blind. In the end, blind and frail, she faces death with dignity and grace.

While some reviewers found the movie too melodramatic, it was generally well-received. According to *The New York Times*, "Miss Davis is superb. More than that, she is enchanted and enchanting. Admittedly it is a great role—rangy, full-bodied, designed for a virtuoso, almost sure to invite the faint damning of tour de force. But that must not detract from the eloquence, the tenderness, the heartbreaking sincerity with which she has played it." Her portrayal of the role earned Bette yet another Oscar nomination. Incidentally, one of her co-stars in *Dark Victory* was none other than future U.S. President Ronald Reagan.

Following *Dark Victory,* Bette made the historical drama *The Private Lives of Elizabeth and Essex*. This film is a fictionalized version of the relationship between Queen Elizabeth I and her favorite, the Earl of Essex, Robert Devereux. It was another movie where Bette would not get her man. Her co-stars were Errol Flynn and Olivia De Havilland. Either Bette or Flynn appeared to be miscast; they were about the same age, but the real Elizabeth I was several decades older than Essex.

Bette didn't want Flynn in the first place. She wanted Laurence Olivier cast as Essex, but because Olivier was still unknown to an American audience, Warner Brothers kept Flynn in the role. Despite her misgivings, Bette did her utmost to prepare for her part, learning as much as she could about Elizabeth I. She even shaved her hair and eyebrows to achieve the Queen's authentic bald look. This was to be Bette's first picture in technicolor, which would splendidly display the colorful costumes.

When the film was released in 1939, the audience responded well to Flynn's roguish performance. The critics, however, were not so kind. According to *The New York Times*, "Bette Davis's Elizabeth is a strong, resolute, glamour-skimping characterization against which Mr. Flynn's Essex has about as much chance as a beanshooter against a tank."

Following *The Private Lives of Elizabeth and Essex,* Bette treated herself to a vacation in New England. That was where she met the man who would become her second husband, Arthur Farnsworth.

Chapter Six

A New England Romance

*"Glamour is so mysterious and fragile. It's a fascination
with the unknown. But how is glamour possible now when
we know everything there is to know about our
celebrities?"*

—Bette Davis

There is no doubt that by 1939, Bette needed to get away
from Hollywood. She and Jack Warner all-to-frequently
disagreed. Still, she was at this point Warner Brothers'
most profitable star, earning a staggering salary of $4,500 a
week. He couldn't just get rid of her. They both agreed that
a break might do them some good.

Bette, having been raised in New England, hoped to
find some solace and peace there. But she wasn't a little
girl anymore. The Hollywood legend tried to visit old
friends and make new acquaintances, but it wasn't easy.
Going home wasn't quite what Bette had hoped for. She
had become more Hollywood than New England, and after
two weeks of wandering, she settled into Peckett's, an inn
and ski resort in Franconia, New Hampshire. The assistant
manager at Peckett's was a handsome, divorced man in his
early thirties named Arthur Farnsworth. He wasn't just an
innkeeper—he was also a pilot and played the violin. Bette
immediately found herself smitten by this cultured and

dashing man. A part of the attraction would have been that he wasn't "Hollywood."

Peckett's provided a number of activities for its guests. One of them was a scenic five-mile trek on horseback through the beautiful countryside. Local legend has it that Bette deliberately got lost so that Farnsworth could find and rescue her. Whatever the case may be, they developed a relationship before Bette had to return to Hollywood to star in her next movie, *The Letter*. By this time, the tabloids had caught on and were in a state of dizziness with constant announcements of an imminent engagement.

As soon as her movie was finished, Bette rushed back to New England and Peckett's Inn. Farnsworth soon proposed, and the couple was promptly wed on December 31, 1940, in Arizona. Since Warner was demanding her presence in Hollywood to shoot *The Great Lie,* they never had a honeymoon. Bette was now dividing her time between Hollywood and New England. She purchased a house from the Peckett family and spent years transforming it into the farm she called Butternut.

To the great delight of the town of Franconia, Bette arranged for the world premiere of *The Great Lie* to happen at the nearby Jax Jr. Theater. Everything was gussied up and prepared for the expected incoming hoard of visitors and elites from Hollywood. Banners announcing the movie were everywhere. Governors from New York and New Hampshire made speeches. New Hampshire had never seen this type of excitement.

Bette and Farnsworth's relationship appeared to work, but sadly, three years into their marriage, Farnsworth collapsed and died from a skull fracture. Bette always insisted that their marriage would have lasted had he not died prematurely. While married to Farnsworth, Bette made one of her most important movies, *The Little Foxes* by Lillian Hellman. In the role of the despicable Regina Hubbard Giddens, the 33-year old Bette was playing the mother of a grown-up daughter, so she once again made sure she wasn't glammed up. It was to be her last movie directed by William Wyler.

The Little Foxes is about greed and power. The Giddens brothers, Oscar and Benjamin, want to buy a cotton mill. To do that, all they need is $75,000 from Regina's husband, Horace. If the deal goes through, Regina will be rich and powerful in her own right. When Horace doesn't provide the money, Oscar suggests a marriage between his son Leo and Horace's daughter Alexandra. This would channel the needed money directly from Horace to Alexandra and thus to Oscar. Regina has no compunction about sacrificing her own child in such a way while Horace is repelled by the suggestion. Regina decides that killing Horace, or rather, letting him die by withholding his medication, is her best option. There is little she won't do to attain wealth and power.

The Little Foxes is a powerful story of the limits to greed, and Bette provides the darkness needed to make such a character believable. The role of Regina, which earned her another Oscar nomination, took so much out of Bette that when it was finished, she traveled to her home in New England to recover.

Chapter Seven

Now, Voyager and All About Eve

"My mother always complimented me. She told me I was pretty, that I had talent, that I was special, and that I could achieve whatever I wanted, if I wanted it enough. All I had to do was to determine what it was I wanted to do, and then to work hard."

—Bette Davis

Bette's next movie *Now, Voyager*, was released in 1942. Like *Dark Victory*, it's a weeper. The movie title is a quote from Walt Whitman, "The untold want by life and land ne'er granted, Now, voyager, sail thou forth, to seek and find." This fairly accurately sums up the movie: life doesn't always grant you what you want, but you must always continue seeking. Thanks to Bette's stellar performance in *Now, Voyager*, she became the first person ever to earn an Oscar nomination five years in a row.

When the movie opens, Charlotte Vale, played by Bette, is an unattractive, unhappy spinster who has been emotionally abused by her socially prominent mother for years. Charlotte is nothing but an embarrassment to the family. Every last vestige of self-esteem that she might once have had is destroyed. She is near a breakdown when her sister-in-law refers her to a psychiatrist, Dr. Jaquith. The doctor has her spend time at a sanitarium, away from her sadistic mother.

As she experiences freedom, Charlotte transforms herself into a lovely woman. With the help of her sister-in-law, she shops for a fashionable wardrobe and sets out on a cruise. At sea, she meets Jerry Duvaux. Jerry is a devoted father and married to a manipulative woman who does not love their daughter. This is something Charlotte can certainly relate to. Charlotte and Jerry eventually fall in love. One of the most memorable and famous scenes is Jerry lighting two cigarettes and then placing one in Charlotte's mouth. There is a strong hint of sensuality between the characters, although the exact nature of their affair remains vague due to the censorship requirements of the times.

When they return to port, they decide it is best for everyone if they no longer see each other. At home, everyone is stunned at how much Charlotte has changed and blossomed. Her mother is not happy with the change since she is afraid of losing control over her daughter. For the first time, Charlotte stands up to her mother and confronts her. Mrs. Vale cannot believe her daughter would dare to question her and dies of a heart attack. Charlotte, filled with guilt, returns to the sanitarium.

At the sanitarium, she meets Jerry's daughter, Tina. Charlotte is immediately drawn to the girl. She knows everything about mothers who do not love their daughters. She is allowed to take Tina home with her and help her heal. Dr. Jaquith and Jerry visit Tina at Charlotte's home, where they find the girl happy and secure. Charlotte agrees to keep Tina as Jerry remains with his invalid wife. Jerry asks Charlotte if that is enough for her. She tells him, "Oh, Jerry, don't let's ask for the moon. We have the stars."

Bette herself continued searching for the stars. In 1945, she met and married her third husband, William Grant Sherry, an artist. With him, she would have her first child in 1947, a daughter named Barbara, better known by her nickname "B. D." Bette continued working throughout these years and was by this point the highest-paid woman in the United States. However, for Bette, the quality of her films was more important than her salary, and so after Warner Brothers refused to grant her script approval, she decided to give up her contract with them after 17 long years.

Now working as a freelancer, Bette enjoyed the freedom of being able to choose her roles, and when she read the script of *All About Eve* in early 1950, she did not hesitate to accept. Filming started in April, and Bette experienced the rare occasion where she ended up with the right man (her co-star Gary Merrill) on-screen. Even better, she and Gary developed a relationship off-screen. Their attraction began when Gary refused to light Bette's cigarette. It was a deliberate (and smart) choice. Too many men in Bette's life had turned into "Mr. Davis," but Gary made it clear from the onset that he had no intention of joining that group. Bette was impressed—and in need.

During the filming of *All About Eve*, Bette was going through a difficult divorce. She had already separated from her husband, William, because of his anger issues and violent outbursts, but the divorce was not finalized until July of 1950. Less than one month later, Bette married

Gary, who became her fourth and final husband. At the age of 42, she told the younger Gary that having children would be unlikely. He was perfectly fine with that. Gary adopted her daughter B. D., and later, the newlyweds adopted a baby girl they called Margot and a boy, Michael.

Sadly, this marriage would not fare any better than Bette's earlier attempts, and there were problems right from the start. While Bette never suspected Gary of cheating, he disappeared for days on end and reappeared a drunken mess. She quickly discovered that in this marriage, alcohol was her rival.

Bette could at least rejoice at the success of *All About Eve*, which received a record 14 Academy Award nominations. In it, Bette plays successful Broadway star Margo Channing. Anne Baxter plays the young, ambitious Eve, who finagles herself into Margo's life by pretending to be a great fan. Gary Merrill plays Margot's lover, Bill, whose proposals she habitually refuses because she is convinced he is in love with the public image of Margo Channing, not who she really is.

There are definite parallels between the aging Bette and the aging Margo in a Hollywood obsessed with youth. After Eve successfully manipulates herself into becoming Margo's understudy, she arranges for Margo to miss a performance and goes on in her stead. Eve has secretly arranged for all important movie critics to be present that evening, especially the caustic Addison DeWitt, who writes a column of the shame of aging actresses clinging to their glory days instead of allowing brilliant new talent, such as Eve, into the theater.

Eve's mission proves successful, and she gets the lead in a play written specifically for Margo. Margo is furious when Eve wins a prestigious acting award. However, she also learns that growing old is inevitable and finally accepts Bill's proposal. She has finally found love. At the end of the movie, Eve, who has connived and lied her way onstage, is approached by a young acting student who pretends to be a fan. Just as Eve has replaced Margo, there are others eager to replace Eve.

Critics and the movie-going audience loved *All About Eve*. Bette may have played the role of Margo with exaggerated drama, but the idea of an aging woman fearing replacement by a younger version had universal appeal.

Chapter Eight

The Horror Years

"Attempt the impossible in order to improve your work."

—Bette Davis

Bette and Gary divorced in 1960 after a tumultuous marriage. When he was drunk, which was a lot of the time, he was likely to resort to violence. According to Bette, *"Offstage, he wasn't perfect, but he was my best husband by far."*

Soon after the divorce, Bette's beloved mother Ruthie died. This left Bette not only heartbroken but also solely responsible for her three children and her sister Bobby, who was prone to mental breakdowns. Add to that, Bette's adopted daughter Margot had special needs and was by this point spending most of her time institutionalized because of brain damage she had received shortly after birth.

Still, work had always come first with Bette. Now in her fifties, she would never again play a spoiled young girl or even an approaching-middle-age role such as Margo Channing. This period saw her transition into horror movies, a genre where youth and beauty weren't of prime importance. Now, Bette was becoming the master at portraying psychotic, older women—and the public loved it. The first of her horror movies is the iconic *What Ever Happened to Baby Jane*, which hit the theaters in October of 1962. For her work in this film, Bette would earn her tenth and final Academy Award nomination.

Many horror films have a plot where helpless, nubile young ladies find themselves in jeopardy from some evil force. It is easy to know who to root for in such a scenario, and the villain is never in doubt. By contrast, *What Ever Happened to Baby Jane* deals with two elderly sisters (played by Bette Davis and Joan Crawford), who were once actresses. Now, they live alone in an old house and have little contact with the outside world. They are both mentally disturbed, and the only question is which one is the most mentally off-balance. Both Bette and Joan allow themselves to be aged with makeup, and Bette especially uses white makeup to make her appear scary and clownish as Baby Jane. There is no hidden monster in the house; it's only two old sisters. The viewer waits with a pounding heart to finds out which of the sister will survive the other.

Baby Jane was such a rousing success that director Robert Aldrich immediately followed it with another pairing of two eerie elderly ladies in *Hush...Hush, Sweet Charlotte*. The movie was about two cousins instead of sisters, and Joan Crawford was initially hired to play Miriam while Bette was set to portray her cousin Charlotte. Bette, however, had no desire to make another film with Crawford, with whom she shared a long-standing rivalry, and was only happy when Crawford was eventually replaced by Olivia de Havilland.

Hush...Hush, Sweet Charlotte proved to be another smash hit. According to *Variety*, "Davis' portrayal is reminiscent of Jane in its emotional overtones, in her style of characterization of the near-crazed former Southern belle, aided by haggard makeup and outlandish attire. It is an outgoing performance, and she plays it to the limit. De Havilland, on the other hand, is far more restrained but nonetheless effective dramatically in her offbeat role."

Next, Bette made *The Nanny* in 1965. In it, she plays the nanny of a boy who has recently returned from being institutionalized because it was thought he drowned his sister years before. In many of her horror movies, Bette gives a no-holds-barred performance, but her performance in *The Nanny* is very subtle and understated. She is cold and reserved, always watching. The understated performance makes Bette especially scary.

Bette continued acting in several more horror movies well into her sixties. Emotionally, she needed to work and keep busy. Also, she had never been obsessed with glamour and was more than willing to appear old, scary, and haggard on the screen. To her, it was just another character to play. Her great rival, Joan Crawford, also tried to conquer the horror movie genre, but without Bette's success. Crawford was an excellent actress, but even in middle age, she could never quite relinquish the need for glamour.

Chapter Nine

The Feud with Joan Crawford

"She has slept with every male star at MGM except Lassie."

—Bette Davis, on Joan Crawford

On a par with the sisterly feud between Olivia de Havilland and Joan Fontaine, Bette Davis and Joan Crawford held a lifetime of animosity toward each other. When Bette began her movie career, Crawford was already famous, and Bette would always insist that Crawford deliberately did all in her power to upstage her. In addition, Crawford had been romantically involved with Clark Gable, a man Bette had wanted for herself.

The final break between the two actresses came when Crawford married Franchot Tone, Bette's co-star in *Dangerous* with whom Bette was madly in love. Bette truly adored Franchot and hoped to marry him. Unfortunately, Crawford, already a major star, invited him to her house for dinner and answered the door naked. It was the end of any Bette-Franchot romance and the beginning of a long, hard feud between two of Hollywood's most iconic actresses. Bette had lost two potential beaus to Crawford—Gable and Franchot—and would never forgive or forget.

Bette eventually became a bigger star than Crawford, much to Crawford's dismay. Their snide remarks about each other became Hollywood legend. They squabbled about everything, from their careers, romances, and their children. According to Crawford, "Poor Bette . . . looks as if there are no happy day, or night, in her life."

Both were well into middle age by the 1960s, and good roles for women that age were rare. They needed a film to keep their careers alive, and it was actually Crawford who approached Bette with the idea of doing *What Ever Happened to Baby Jane*. Bette, also worried about her career, agreed to do the movie. This was the first time Bette and Crawford had worked together on the same film. Professional rivalry soon shifted into all-out war.

Contrary to Bette, who rarely cared about the opinions of others, Crawford felt a need to be liked. When the shooting for *Baby Jane* began, Joan sent the crew gifts in an effort to win them to her side. Bette wrote her a note telling her to, "Get off the crap!" The movie contains a scene where Baby Jane (Bette) beats up her sister Blanche (Crawford). Crawford suspected Bette might play rough, and she was right. Bette hit her hard on the head. When Crawford yelped in pain, Bette blinked innocently. "I barely touched her."

The tables were turned the following week. In a scene where Baby Jane drags Blanche out of a room, Crawford turned herself into dead weight to be as heavy as possible. She even wore a heavy weightlifter's belt underneath her dress. Crawford was perfectly aware that Bette suffered from back pain and that this scene would be excruciating for her. While Bette cried in agony, Crawford casually retired to her dressing room as if she had no idea what had just happened.

The situation worsened after the film was finished. Crawford fumed when Bette, not she, received an Oscar nomination for their movie. Everyone thought Bette would win the Best Actress award, and she herself was so sure that she stubbed out her cigarette before her category was read. Bette did not win however. If that wasn't bad enough, Crawford rushed past her saying, "Excuse me, I have an Oscar to collect." Bette was unaware that Crawford had arranged a deal with the other nominated actresses who were not able to be there in person to pick up the award. That evening, Crawford picked up the Oscar for the absent winner, Anne Bancroft. Therefore, it was she who went on stage and into the spotlight instead of Bette.

Bette and Crawford never filmed together again. Of the two women, Crawford was first to die. Bette's only comment was, "You should never say bad things about the dead, only good… Joan Crawford is dead. Good."

Bette was also getting up in years, but because she needed the money, especially for Margot's sanitarium expenses, she continued to work. In her later years, she did plays and made guest appearances on television as well as starred in films.

Chapter Ten

My Mother's Keeper

"If you have never been hated by your child, you have never been a parent."

—Bette Davis

In 1978, Joan Crawford's adopted daughter Christina shocked Hollywood and the rest of the world with her book *Mommie Dearest,* which describes the abuse Christina and her brother had endured at the hands of Crawford. It was difficult for fans to imagine a Hollywood icon beating her daughter with coat hangers, but readers bought the book in droves while critics debated the actual facts. If Bette felt any sense of schadenfreude at seeing her rival trashed and humiliated, the elation wouldn't last long.

Seven years later, Bette's daughter B. D. would come out with her own story, *My Mother's Keeper.* B. D. paints a vivid picture of Bette as a sarcastic, neurotic drunk who abused her fragile sister Bobby and her own grandchildren. The fact that Bette could be difficult was well-known, and many of the people who worked in her movies attested to the tense working conditions she could create on a set. Nevertheless, she had always been presented as a devoted mother, sister, and grandmother.

B. D. was utterly brutal in her depiction of her mother. With a mother as busy as Bette, it was undoubtedly difficult to provide a normal childhood for her children. B. D. appeared especially traumatized by Gary Merrill, who was known for his violent outbursts. Theirs was obviously an erratic and dysfunctional household. Strangely, B. D. blamed the fights, beatings, and screaming on her mother, saying, "If Mother had minded Gary's attacks and all the violence, she would have done something about it." At the age of 16, B. D. married 29-year-old film executive Jeremy Hyman. According to her book, Bette was jealous of her marriage and worked hard at breaking them up, although the marriage lasted for more than 50 years.

Most of the allegations presented in the book have since been denounced as false, but whatever the facts, *My Mother's Keeper* is a sad book. The pain of a neglected daughter springs from every page. It is a fact that Bette always put her career first, although much of that was out of necessity to support herself and her family. As difficult as she could be, she had always loved and provided for her family.

My Mother's Keeper became a bestseller, and it revealed family wounds and pain to the world. Its publication crashed Bette's world. Bette was too embarrassed to go to a bookstore and purchase the book herself, so she sent a friend to pick up a copy instead. After reading it, she disinherited B. D. and her grandchildren. It was a situation where everyone suffered and no one won. Bette and B. D. never spoke again.

Bette's only response to B. D.'s accusations came in her memoir published in 1987. The last chapter of *This 'n That* deals with the sense of betrayal she felt about her daughter's story and contains an open letter to B. D. In it, she says that "The sum total of your having written this book is a glaring lack of loyalty and thanks for the very privileged life I feel you have been given."

Conclusion

Bette grew frail with age. By the time *My Mother's Keeper* was published, Bette had suffered several strokes and become unbearably thin due to her battle with breast cancer. Still, vanity demanded that she dress well and wore makeup in public, which she always did. In 1989, Bette attended the San Sebastian Film Festival, despite her physical infirmities. She collapsed and was rushed to the American Hospital in Neuilly, France. There was no hope for a recovery. As efficient as ever, Bette spent her last days on the telephone putting her affairs in order, including canceling a lunch appointment for the following week.

Bette Davis died on October 6, 1989. She was 81 years old. During her 60-year career, she made nearly 100 movies, many of which have become classics. She received ten Oscar nominations and won two of them. In 1977, she was the first woman to be honored with the American Film Institute's Lifetime Achievement Award. Few actresses have lasted in Hollywood for six decades. One of the reasons that Bette Davis did is that she was always willing to play unlikeable characters which other actresses shied away from. She never relied on her good looks to succeed—instead, raw talent and hard work saw her rise where many others had fallen. It is not hard to believe Bette Davis when she said, "I survived because I was tougher than anybody else."

Made in United States
North Haven, CT
20 October 2022

25681944R00024